C000060568

# My Puppet
# Art Class

Nellie Shepherd

A Dorling Kindersley Book

LONDON, NEW YORK, MUNICH, MELBOURNE, AND DELHI

Editor Penny Smith
Designer Wendy Bartlet
Managing Art Editor Diane Thistlethwaite
Production Rochelle Talary
Photography Stephen Hepworth


For Chris Harris (A Wonderful Person!)

ACKNOWLEDGEMENTS
With thanks to: Jean Gollner, Anne Lumb, Wendy Morrison,
James Pendrich, Melena and Megan Smart (MMKS Logistics), Joan Fallows,
David Hansel (Memery Crystal), and the children from Cressbrook Mill,
Abbeydale School, and Broomhall Nursery School and Early Years Centre.
Special thanks to the artists: Peggy Atherton, Emma Hardy,
Donna Huddleston, Amy McSimpson, Lynne Moulding
and Emma Parsons.

First published in Great Britain in 2003
by Dorling Kindersley Limited
80 Strand, London WC2R ORL
A Penguin Company
2 4 6 8 10 9 7 5 3 1

See
Dorling Kindersley's
complete catalogue at
www.dk.com

Text and materials copyright © 2003 Nellie Shepherd
'Nellie's' is a trademark of Nellie Shepherd

Illustration and compilation copyright © 2003 Dorling Kindersley Limited, London

All rights reserved. No part of this publication may be reproduced,
stored in a retrieval system, or transmitted in any form or by any
means, electronic, mechanical, photocopying, recording, or otherwise,
without the prior written permission of the copyright owner.

A CIP catalogue record for this book
is available from the British Library

ISBN: 1-4053-0082-5

Colour reproduction by GRB Editrice, Italy
Printed and bound in Italy by L.E.G.O.

# Where to find things

# My Puppet Art Class

This book is all about making gorgeous puppets – and you can play with them, too!

The process of making and playing with puppets releases enormous amounts of imagination and creativity. It is a fantastic learning and developing experience! All the puppets have their own characters and personalities. My favourite pastime is swanning around, so I love making Serena Swan best! Go for it!

Nellie Shepherd

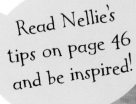

Read Nellie's tips on page 46 and be inspired!

4

# Basic Kit

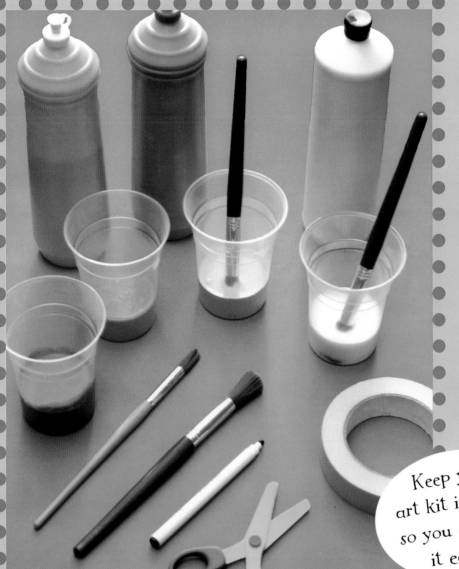

As well as the equipment pictured with each project, you will need the following basic kit:

| | |
|---|---|
| card | pots (for paint |
| paper | and glue) |
| paints | paintbrushes |
| felt-tip pens | rollers |
| pencils | tissue paper |
| PVA glue | cotton wool |
| tape (masking | wool |
| tape is best) | beads |
| scissors | |
| stapler | |

Keep your art kit in a box so you can find it easily!

# Helping hand

All the projects in this book are designed for young children to make, but they should only be attempted under adult supervision. Extra care should be taken when using sharp equipment, such as scissors, staplers, and pipe cleaners, and with small objects that may cause choking. Only use PVA or other non-toxic, water-soluble glue.

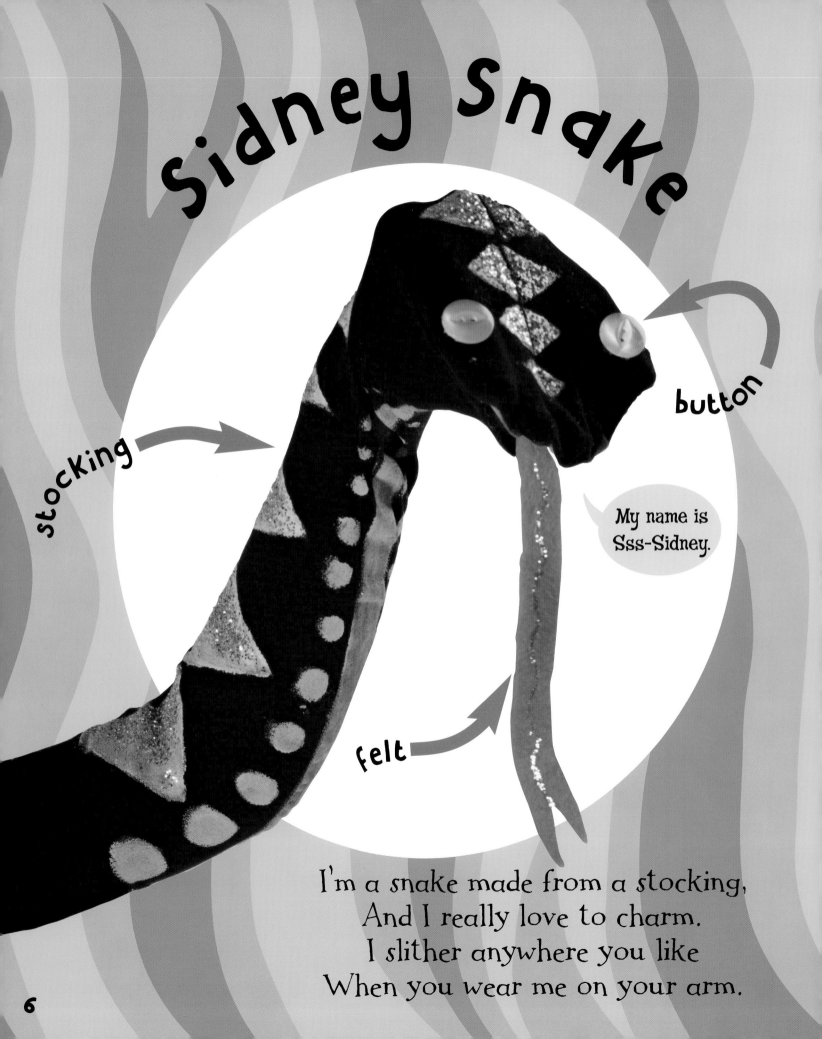

# Sidney Snake

stocking

button

felt

My name is
Sss-Sidney.

I'm a snake made from a stocking,
And I really love to charm.
I slither anywhere you like
When you wear me on your arm.

6

# You can use...

glue

glitter

paint

shiny things

stocking or pop sock

buttons

card

felt

# How to make it!

## pull

Cut out a long strip of card slightly narrower than your stocking (or pop sock). Pull your stocking over the card. Now you can paint your stocking and it won't stick together.

## paint

Mix paint with some glue. Paint zigzags, spots, stripes, or any other pattern on your stocking to make your very own Sidney Snake. Stick on glitter and other shiny things.

## glue

Glue on Sidney's red felt tongue and button eyes. Pull out the strip of card before your stocking sticks to it.

## play!

It's lots of fun playing with your Sidney Snake – and he keeps you warm, too!

8

Did you know? Snakes never stop growing. When their skin becomes too tight, they slide out of it. There is a new skin underneath!

# Elsie the Elephant

paper plate

card

I'm Elsie
The Elephant,
And I love to play.
But that isn't very easy
As my ears
Get in the way!

# You can use...

paper plates

glue

glitter

card

**Tot Tip!** Don't worry if you've run out of paper plates. Just cut out a circle from stiff card and use that instead.

# Here we go!

## cut out

Cut out two card ear shapes like the one shown below. Staple them to a paper plate to make Elsie's head and her lovely flappy ears. Staple half a plate to the back of Elsie's head, so it sticks out to make a handle.

## fold

Cut out a long trunk shape from card. Fold the card backwards and forwards to make Elsie's concertina-like trunk.

## glue

Glue or tape Elsie's trunk to her paper-plate head – her trunk bounces up and down nicely! Glue on Elsie's card face, and add glitter to make her sparkle.

**Did you know?**
Real elephants like to flap their great big ears to help keep themselves cool!

# You can use...

card

glue

tissue paper

coloured paper

glitter

paper fasteners

cork

wiggly eye

feathers

## Tot Tip!

Use garden canes to hold up your Percy Parrot. You can buy them at gardening shops.

15

# How to make it!

## copy

Copy this picture of Percy onto card and cut it out. Cut out Percy's beak pieces and his wing separately.

*Nice cutting out!*

## stick

Brush glue over Percy's body and wing. Stick on multi-coloured paper shapes, feathers, and of course glitter! Make his eye from a cork and a wiggly eye. Decorate his beak, too!

## join

Join Percy's beak and wing to his body using paper fasteners. Now these pieces can move up and down!

## tape

Tape a garden cane along the back of Percy's body. Tape another cane along his wing and make him fly!

16

Kid's talk
"Parrots talk
a lot, just
like me."
Alex, age 3

19

# You can use...

glue

black fabric

elastic band

wool

pipe cleaners

card

shiny moon

garden cane

wiggly eyes

cotton wool

stars

## Tot Tip!

For Mr Sparks' body, you need to cut a cone from card and a robe from black fabric. Use the shapes below as a guide.

card cone

fabric robe

19

# You can do it!

## stick

For Mr Sparks' body, tape together your card cone. Stick black fabric round the cone, leaving enough at the open end for his robe.

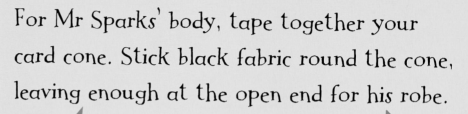

## scrunch

Make Mr Sparks' head by scrunching gluey tissue paper into a ball. Use more glue and tissue paper to stick the head onto a garden cane.

## gather

Push the cane right through the cone. Gather the robe fabric under Mr Sparks' head and secure it with an elastic band. Stick on his eyes, wool hair, and cotton-wool beard.

## Wrap

For Mr Sparks' arms, simply wrap a pipe cleaner round his body. To finish, glue on a moon and stars, a card hat, and a little wand.

**Kid's talk**
"I pull the stick
and Mr Sparks
goes away."
Sally, age 4

# Kitty and Noodle

We're two little friends
Made from envelopes.
Our names
Are Kitty and Noodle.
Making us is such fun,
And when you're done,
You'll have a black cat
And a poodle!

straws

tissue paper

22

# You can use...

glue

glitter

ribbon

envelopes

straws

wiggly eyes

tissue paper

card

**Tot Tip!**

You don't need new envelopes for Kitty and Noodle. Make them from old, used ones if you like – it's a great way to recycle!

23

# Here We go!

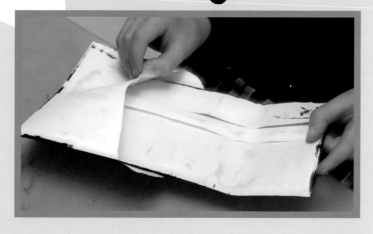

## Kitty

For Kitty, slot one long envelope into a smaller one to make a 'T' shape. Secure it with tape. Then cut a strip off the bottom of the 'T' for your hand to go in.

## stick

Stick on Kitty's card ears, then paint her all over. Glue on eyes, a nose, and a mouth all made of card, and straw whiskers. We also gave our Kitty card inner ears, a ribbon collar, and a bit of glitter!

## Noodle

For Noodle, paint a long envelope in a lovely bright colour. Cut a pointy chin shape at one end of the envelope.

## cover

Stick on pieces of card for the top of Noodle's head and her ears. Cover them in tissue-paper balls. Stick on wiggly eyes, and use card for her eyebrows, nose, and mouth. Put glittery bows in her hair.

# Serena Swan

I'm Serena Swan,
And I look very grand.
I swim around
So gracefully
When you wave
Your hand.

I like swanning around.

sock

feathers

paper plate

# You can use...

glue

feathers

shiny shapes

pipe cleaner

wiggly eyes

felt-tipped pen

paint

sock

paper plates

net fabric

flowers

**Tot Tip!**

For Serena's feathers you can cut a little bit off a cheap feather boa (no one will notice!) or use tissue paper instead.

# How to make it!

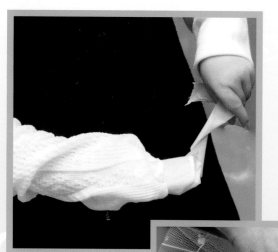

## tape

Put the sock on your hand and make Serena's beak by taping round your fingers. Use paint or felt-tipped pen to colour her beak.

## twist

For Serena's eyes, twist a pipe cleaner round her beak and stick a wiggly eye and shiny shape on each end.

## staple

For her wings, fold four paper plates in half. Staple two of the plates together to make a bracelet that fits your arm. Staple the other two plates to the bracelet to look like wings.

## play

Decorate Serena with feathers or tissue paper. We gave Serena a net headdress with little flowers. To play, pull on your Serena sock, slide the wing bracelet over the top, and have fun!

**Kid's talk**
"Swans are ducks
with long necks."
Clare, age 4

# Bella the Butterfly

pipe cleaner

washing-up brush

paper plate

I'm Bella the Butterfly.
I flutter in the trees,
Then fly down to the flowers
To chatter with the bees!

# You can use...

glue

paper plates

pom poms

glitter

paint

pipe cleaners

card

washing-up brush

tissue paper

sequins

**Tot Tip!**

Instead of a washing-up brush, you can use a toothbrush and make a baby Bella the Butterfly. Cut out her mini wings from card.

# You can do it!

Fly high!

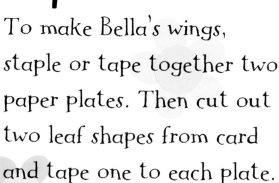

## tape

To make Bella's wings, staple or tape together two paper plates. Then cut out two leaf shapes from card and tape one to each plate.

## paint

Have fun decorating Bella's wings! Paint a pattern on one wing, then press the second wing onto the wet paint to make it match.

## twist

Tape on a washing-up brush to make Bella's body. Twist on pipe-cleaner antennae and add a pom-pom eye on each.

## stick

You can stick tissue paper to Bella's wings and add a tissue-paper fantasy tail. Glue on sequins and glitter to make her pretty. Then wave Bella up and down and watch her fly!

32

### Kid's talk

"My butterfly flutters. It goes flut, flut, flut, when you shake it."
Helena, age 3 ½

# Fingers and Thumbs

We're a group of puppet pals.
Come and check us out.
Put us on your fingers
And wiggle us about!

# You can use...

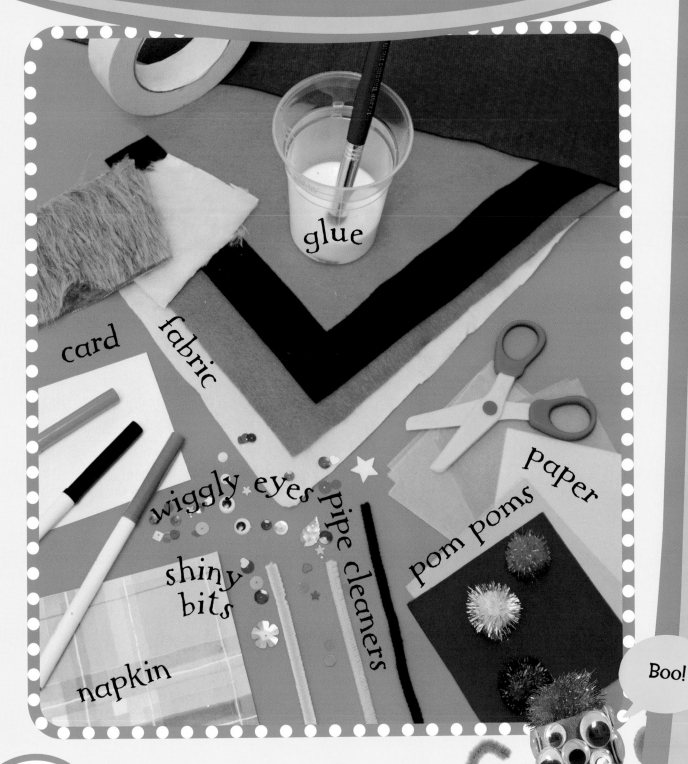

glue

card

fabric

wiggly eyes

pipe cleaners

paper

shiny bits

pom poms

napkin

Boo!

**Tot Tip!** You can use all sorts of materials to make your puppets wacky and individual – wool, paper, shiny beads and sequins, cotton wool, and lots more!

# Here We go!

## roll

Finger puppets are so easy to make and such fun to play with! To make a puppet's body, roll an oblong of card into a tube that fits over your finger. Secure it with tape.

## make a puppy...

There are so many ways to decorate your puppet's body – you can glue on cotton-wool fur, card ears, and wiggly eyes to make a puppy.

## ...or a lady

Or try making a lovely lady by sticking on wool hair, a bead mouth, and wiggly eyes. Add a fabric or napkin skirt held in place with pipe-cleaner arms.

I love that green hair!

## make it up!

Here's a handful of puppets we've made. You can copy ours, or make up your own – and remember, anything goes!

Thumbs up for me!

Kid's talk
"I've got friends
on my fingers."
Alex, age 3 ½

# Chi Chi the Dragon

I'm such fun to make!

plastic fork

chopstick

paper plate

I'm Chi Chi the Dragon
And I come from China.
I dance up and down –
There's no dragon finer!

# You can use...

glue

tinsel

glitter

paint

paper

paper plates

plastic fork

chopsticks

paper fasteners

tissue paper

# How to make it!

## decorate

First, decorate five or more paper plates to make Chi Chi's head and body. Try using paint, glitter, or tissue paper.

## join

Join together your decorated plates using paper fasteners – attach the rim of one plate to near the middle of the next.

Nice tinsel beard!

## stick

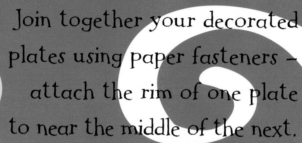

Stick on Chi Chi's face – a tinsel beard and paper eyes, nose, and tongue work perfectly! Add horns and a tail cut from more painted plates.

## tape

Tape on plastic forks to make Chi Chi's legs. Then make handles to hold by taping one chopstick to Chi Chi's head and another to her bottom.

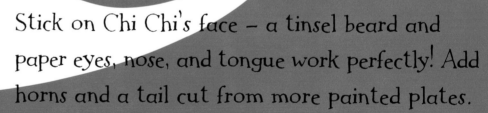

**Did you know?**
In China, the dragon stands for long life and riches. People celebrate the Chinese New Year by performing with giant dragon puppets!

# Show Time!

tissue paper

Squawk! Hi,
I'm Percy!

Now you've got
Some puppets,
It's time
To have a go
At making
A grand theatre,
And putting
On a show!

Hello!
I'm Serena
Swan!

cardboard
box

# You can use...

glue

card

paint

tissue paper

string

pegs

**Tot Tip!**

For this theatre, you need two big boxes that are about the same size. If you don't have any, ask at your local supermarket.

# You can do it!

## cut

Your theatre is made from two boxes stacked on top of each other. Cut the back and top off the lower box. Cut the front, back, and bottom off the upper box. Tape the boxes together.

## cover

Cover your theatre with tissue paper. Use a rag or roller to add lots of bright paint. Cut out a little peep hole in the lower box.

## make curtains

To make curtains, run string across the front window of the theatre and tape it in place. Fold tissue paper over the string and staple to hold. Slide the tissue-paper curtains along the string to open them.

## finish

To finish, you can tape a card crown to the top of your theatre, stick on tissue-paper flowers, or clip on pegs covered in glitter. Then it's showtime!

**Kid's talk**
"Don't sit on the boxes or you'll squash the play."
Max, age 3 ½

# Nellie's Knowledge

I've been teaching my art class to children for over ten years. Along the way, I've discovered a few tips that make the classes brilliant fun – and help bring out the creativity in all of us!

## Organisation
It's good to have all the things you need before you start. But if you haven't got something, just improvise and use something else!

## Make it last!
Use extra masking tape to give your puppets longer life. This tape is brilliant as you can decorate on top of it!

## Fun factor!
Think about inviting friends over to join in. Play music and have a story break. It makes such a difference.

## Making mess

Art is a messy business! Just put down lots of newspaper, relax, and create. It's worth it!

## Encouragement

Encouragement is great for building confidence and creativity: one hundred percent encouragement equals one hundred percent creativity!

## Positive attitude

We're positive! In my art classes we never say we can't do something because we simply can!

## Making choices

Children's concentration is greatest when they choose the things they want to make. They make their own decisions from the start and they see them through.

## Playtime!

Let children play with their art. It releases imagination and is the best fun ever!

We've had lots of fun. Curtains!